Forests of the [K]Night

Richard Jesson

Published by Richard Jesson, 2016.

Forests of the [K]night

A Play in One or Two Acts
by
Richard Jesson
©2010

Ty Cobb visits Ernest Hemingway in 1960
a biographical fantasy

FORESTS OF THE [K]NIGHT

First edition. July 5, 2016.

Copyright © 2016 Richard Jesson.

ISBN: 979-8224829453

Written by Richard Jesson.

Introductory Note

More than chronological coincidence brings together Ty Cobb and Ernest Hemingway, who never met, in this play set in late 1960. Cobb was dying of cancer and other ailments but still driving himself around the country, and Hemingway had been admitted to the Mayo Clinic, ostensibly for hypertension and other physical ailments but actually for what might now be diagnosed as bi-polar disorder with strong suicidal tendencies. They died about eight months later in July of 1961. Here are some of the biographical similarities.

Both came from well educated middle class families. Cobb's father was an academic and politician; Hemingway's, a doctor.

Both lost their fathers just as they were starting their careers. Hemingway's father shot himself; Cobb's father, mistaken for a prowler, was shot by his wife (Cobb's mother).

Both, by dedication and discipline quickly rose to the highest levels of their professions. Each had a much less disciplined rival: in baseball George Herman (Babe) Ruth, in writing Francis Scott Key (F. Scott) Fitzgerald.

Both were outdoorsmen and familiar with guns, rods, and reels throughout their lives. Both on occasion fought with their fists.

Both experienced inevitable decline in their abilities. Cobb retired from baseball, after a final year in which he batted a mere .323, and continued to manage and charitably distribute his healthy income from stock investments, while Hemingway, though suffering constant frustration from his mental confusion, attempted to write until he took his life with one of his shotguns.

The "action" is Hemingway's manic-depressive journey through ups (when he is distracted by various "games," one involving a shotgun) and downs (dwelling on his failures) to a temporary calm as he is led off to electroconvulsive therapy – or, to the hidden shotgun. What happens? Historically, Hemingway did undergo ECT, and he did shoot himself.

As they see him for the last time, the audience must judge if he is more up than down and if, at least for the moment, he is responsive to the love and concern of the other characters, and of his off-stage wife.

THE CHARACTERS

H[EMINGWAY] ◈ white male, early 60s but appears older, about six foot, heavy build

C[OBB] ◈ white male, early 70s, six foot, medium build

NURSE ◈ white female, 35-45, middle height/build

MORT ◈ black male, late teens to early 20s, middle height/build (looks, and actually is, fast)

SET

A residence room at St. Mary's Hospital, the Mayo Clinic, Rochester, MN. A dresser (paper, pencils, books on top, chest-high to H), single bed, bed-side table (shot glass and bottles of Jim Beam and Johnny Walker), two chairs, small stove. Monochrome walls, minimal decorations: a crucifix and one picture (Hemingway loved "The Gulf Stream" by Winslow Homer). Open doors leading out of room on each side (see below) and a door with mirror to bathroom stage left.

OFFSTAGE

Right is building's entrance, reception, public halls, nurses' stations, other patients' rooms, closets, etc.

Left is offices, labs, treatment (as ECT) rooms.

TIME

Late Fall, 1960, a weekday.

Note on Language: The play contains some common swear words, used by C and H between themselves and in one scene between H and Nurse. C and H avoid "bad language" when Mort is present, sometimes changing a word in mid-speech.

Lights or Curtain Up

[H in robe and pajamas stands writing on dresser, crosses out a word, writes another, looks at last line, lifts sheet briefly to look at bottom of one under it, moves pencil to top of top sheet and counts with it, about 50 motions. PA offstage paging Dr. Romm. H puts down pencil, smoothes edges of the stack, looks at it. He takes off and lays down his glasses, places his hands on the sides of the dresser top and slowly lowers his forehead to it. Hold for three beats. He pulls back violently, wrenching the dresser top towards him so that books, etc., fall off the top, roaring:]

H: One-eighty! [kicks book or other object]

NURSE: [enters quickly with a folder, which she puts down near bed as she picks other things, but not papers, off floor] Mr. Hemingway! What have you done?

H: What?! Not enough!

[H paces behind nurse, glances down at folder]

MORT: [entering] What's the matter?

H: Words, words, words …

MORT: [picking up sheets of paper] Your writing.

NURSE: You're writing every day at this time.

H: Shhh[as H changes the obscenity, with his foot he slides folder under bed]oot!

N/M: Calm/Easy. [Nurse approaches to check pulse at H's wrist, but waved off.]

H: Alright! I need a drink! [sits on bed and partakes of bottle] One hundred eighty words! I'm batting friggin' one-eighty. If I were master of my craft, it would probably be one-fifty.

MORT: Oh, Mr. H, a hundred of your words are worth fifty by anyone else.

H: Ha! You're just trying to make me feel better. I have to do better. What's wrong with me?

[From top drawer of chest, which has slid open, Mort takes a cardboard box and hides it in his orderly's jacket as he closes drawer.]

NURSE: Well, you are still drinking, which—

H: Thank God for small favors. [drink]

NURSE:—is not a behavior beneficial to your intellectual endeavors. And some mental as well as physical deficit does often result from having been in small aircraft which descend too abruptly.

H: Oh, lordy, why I can't I write like that? Does Milady suggest that the rococo nature of my nonwriting life has impaired my ability to produce masterpieces of minimalist fiction?

NURSE: [hands H glasses] That could be one way of putting it. [looks around room—something bothering her but all looks neat—enumerates objects now replaced on dresser:] Bible, Oxford Book of English Verse, pencil, paper, stapler.

H: Stones and mortar of civilization. Along with your hair pins and my belt.

MORT: "Gott mit uns."

H: Amen.

NURSE: Anyway, perhaps that is an end of the writing for today?

H: For today ... an end ...

NURSE: And there are still breakfast trays [H shakes head.] if you wish to supplement that liquid diet. [H simply scowls at her. Nurse exits. Mort perhaps would like to make bed, but H is sitting on it.]

H: Never happened to me, kid; happened to other people—Scott ...

MORT: Who?

H: He could spin 'em out. Spun out himself. Francis Scott Key Fitzgerald. [Mort still looks puzzled.] F. Scott to you.

MORT: Oh, I've heard that name. You know him?

H: All the good writers. Him, one of the first, used to visit me in Paris.

MORT: Maybe he could visit you here, talk about writing?

H: That may be the miracle I need.

MORT: O.K., tell the doctors! They can get in touch with him.

H: Uh-huh. Old son-of-a-gun died twenty years ago.

MORT: Oh, I'm sorry. I know how that is. He must have been like a father to you.

H: Two, three years older. Senseless waste ... . Well, he's covered, six feet under; a fair explanation of why the great American reading public has no new best-seller from the silver typewriter of fabulous Frank.

MORT: Ahh. [sympathetic sound]

H: Where am I?

MORT: St. Mary's, Mr. H.

H: I'm up Short Creek without an excuse. You'll have to be mine: get out, I can't think with all these people around!

MORT: Yes, sir, I'll check if it's time for any medicine.

H: Out! [H snaps fingers of right hand which finishes with finger pointing at Mort, who leaves.] As if there were alibis for not writing anything as good as you can. [PA paging Dr. Serling.] O.K., boss. [H lifts mattress, pulls out a shotgun and examines it]

MORT: [knocks offstage] Mr. H ...

H: Not now, Mort.

MORT: [still offstage] That's O.K., I just came to tell you you don't have to take any medicine now.

H: Right. So long.

MORT: Bye then.

H: [shakes his head] Mort. O.K. [looks at gun again then uses it to fish under bed and slide out file; he puts gun back under mattress, picks up and opens folder, lays it on bed] Yup, as expected, but [puts on glasses] let's see if there are any surprises. [sits on bed and leafs through papers, muttering] .. "[(under breath)sixty-one-year]-old male ... admitted ... history:" That's how she'd know about the old plane crash—crashes. "damaged knee ... cracked discs ... dislocated shoulder ... ruptured liver, right kidney—oh, yeah!—spleen ... damaged nerve [scanning page] 'nerve,' singular? ... [turns page] arms, face, head burned ...hearing, eyes ... lumbar vertebrae, diabetes mellitus," bunch of Latin and Greek words meaning "bad." Answers? Not the answer. " ... blah,

blah, fractured skull-slash-brain," hell yes! I was trapped in a burning plane and had to butt my way out. "Anemia, hypertension ... concussion ... concussion ... concussion." [There is a pen on a string attached to the file; H takes it and writes] "X-rays of ... patient's head ... reveal nothing."

[knocking stage right]

MORT: Mr. H?

H: What now?

MORT: Just my cleaning.

H: [conceals file] Yeah, yeah.

MORT: [entering] O.K. [Mort brings pail with cleaners, sponge, toilet paper, newspaper to front of stage, puts it down, takes out Windex and sprays quickly about shoulder height toward audience.] You have a nice view, Mr. H.

H: Mhmhph.

MORT: [starts wiping with crumpled newspaper—sound effects optional] You can see the woods. Mostly evergreens. Pretty dark now. But you must have had a few trees with nice colors back in October.

H: Mort!

MORT: What?!

H: You were here when I came!

MORT: Oh, yeah.

H: And I'm not gonna be around next fall.

MORT: What!?! Oh! Yeah, you'll be out of here before you know it. We'll miss you.

H: Hmph.

MORT: [with pail moves towards bathroom] I've got more toilet paper in case you need it. [no response; Mort cleans mirror on bathroom door] Probably you don't. [no response] I'll see.

H: [mutter] Yeah.

MORT: [turns toward H] Mary's always bringing new toilet paper to the women's rooms. I almost never need more. I don't understand.

H: Hummph. Maybe Mary can explain it.

MORT: Maybe so. [opens bathroom door] I'll ask her. I'm going to shut the door now. I won't make much noise, but I'll shut the door.

H: Mmmph.

[Mort in bathroom shuts door. Knocking stage right]

H: [rises, opens bottom drawer of dresser and tosses in file] It's open. [closes drawer; no response] ... This is a private room, but they want my suicide, should I choose to perform it, to be semi-private, therefore it is always open.

C: [formal] May I come in?

H: [mock formal] Who is it who inquires?

C: "The greatest of all ballplayers and an absolute shit," [entering] end quote.

H: Mr. Tyrus Raymond Cobb.

C: Ty. [They shake hands.] H: Ernie. C: Right.

H: No offense meant.

C: None given by the compliment.

H: No compliment; a judgment, in which many concurred.

C: [nods appreciation] Many agreed with the insult, because I beat them. A few no doubt applied similar epithets to you.

H: And not always because I beat them. A couple of wives for instance.

C: That's about my handicap.

H: And what brings the old Johnny Reb back north?

C: East. I'm living in Nevada. [muted sound of toilet flushing]

H: God-forsaken place, ain't it?

C: Well, the godless keep the taxes down.

H: Ha! I may have to look into that. I'm losing a lot by not being able to work in Cuba. If I stay too long in Idaho, the taxes are going to kill me.

C: Alright. Here's a reminder for you. [C takes silver dollar out of pocket and hands it to H.]

H: Hey, thanks. D'you remember where and when you got it?

C: This particular one? [hint at this point that C begins to see H as a bit crazy]

H: Yeah.

C: No, they're all over the place out there. I carry around a few when I travel; they're a curiosity for most people now.

H: O.K. So [putting coin in robe pocket—both sit]—what brings you east?

C: Much the same as you, I suppose: a few tests.

H: Sorry to hear that …

C: Cancer.

H: Very sorry. I hope they find it and fry it.

C: Thank you. I believe they're trying to make my remaining organs radioactive.

H: I believe they want to throw an electrical charge into all my brain cells. If we get together, we might power half the households in your godforsaken state.

BOTH: It won't work.

C: Well, we'll see.

H: Then we'll see.

C: In the meantime [takes a drink].

H: Saludo [raises bottle but does not drink—Mort comes out of bathroom; H gestures:] Mort. Mr. Cobb.

MORT: Cobb?

C: Ty Cobb.

MORT: Mr. Ty Cobb? [H nods.] Wow. Mr. Cobb, I'm Mort.

C: [rises briefly to shake hands] Good, old-fashioned name. I knew a pitcher named Mort.

MORT: Oh.

H: More than old, ominous. Means "death."

MORT: [grimaces slightly] No, it's just short for—

C: Thank you, professor; my education wasn't as wide as yours, but we did study Latin in my day. Mors mortis morti mortem nisi morte dedisset. I forget the Latin for the other verse.

H: Me too.

[Both together]

H: The doors of heaven were—

C: The gates of life were—[Both stop.]

H: O.K. "Gates of life" is good. The [C joins in] gates of life were closed to our crying / Had not death's foe put death to death by dying.

MORT: Wow, what's that?

H: That's a play on your name, from Latin, mors mortis morti mortem ...

MORT: Wow.

C: Only a "play."

H: [to C] One of my wives put our sons in a private school back east. Every year some parents went to the headmaster complaining that their boys had to waste time learning a dead language. He'd listen and then tell them, "You're not the first to bring this up, and [H mimes reaching in drawer and holding up paper] I've found three schools in the next two counties where your sons could go and have no Latin requirement." Ha! how do you like that, gentlemen?

C: They came to make him choose, and he gave them a choice.

H: Which was no choice. Darn right. This was his job; they weren't going to tell him how to do it. You don't mess with the master.

[During next exchange, C grimaces in pain, pulls flask from jacket, and drinks.]

MORT: And he was the headmaster.

H: Hey, kid, you have at least two things going for you: you pay attention, and you're quick.

C: And two against. [C gestures with flask to include H and himself.] Now you know us.

MORT: Oh, yes, now. Are you going to be around for a little bit, Mr. Cobb?

C: One way or another.

MORT: I'd really like it if you could do something for me, as soon as I do one more room. [C nods.] Thanks! See you soon. [Exit, stage right.]

C: So, young man, what have you been doing to wind up here at your early age? I hear you hang out with the players down on the Gulf. They knock you over too many times?

H: Ha, you've heard stories. I can't tell them. I may have been a little drunker than the ballplayers I challenged to box, but I don't think I got myself batted around too much—probably went down with one punch.

C: That's about what I heard.

H: Can't say much for today's ballplayers. I'm afraid they're getting refined.

C: Certainly compared to my day. When I began playing the game, baseball was about as gentlemanly as a kick in the crotch.

H: So you fit right in.

C: Oh, no, that was just it. A certain faction on my own team didn't accept a young southern gentleman and tried to run me off. Yankee Micks, Catholics, no offense.

H: None taken. I'm familiar with both breeds. [C not sure] Irish Catholics, southern gentlemen.

C: Yeah. Tough guys and hotheads. If the season had been a week longer they might have succeeded. I can't say they put the demon in me, but they brought it out; and did me an unintended favor, drove me off by myself with time to think.

H: That is a favor. Uninterrupted time by yourself to think—I could use more of that.

C: I don't want to impose myself. Tell the kid—

H: No, no, please stay. Don't think I'm doing any more work today, and I prefer to have company when I'm not working. And maybe your talk might suggest a story. Sometimes it falls in a writer's lap that way. So rookie had to fight back or clear out, survival of the fiercest.

C: That's about it. I survived. Still doing so, barely. And you …

H: Mind not running so good, but I'm not in bad shape: a little excess flab, hypertension, and supposed not to engage in too much of this action [indicates bottle but does not drink], but liver, cholesterol good. Blood pressure not so good, but getting it down along with my weight. That's the drill.

C: Should pan out. Not a bad setup here. And you say you're still writing?

H: Have to. It's like physical exercise, I need to do it to keep going.

C: And … right here?

H: [gestures to dresser] Standing up, old habit. But that's a bit of a sore subject.

C: Standing?

H: Writing.

C: Ah, a painful area. [grimaces and drinks]

H: Helluva situation. This may help with the pain [lifts bottle but doesn't drink], but I've been told, and observed, that it doesn't help with the writing. The mind has to be clear, and free of … only wrote two hours, page and a half today. But, … Life Magazine sent me to Spain last year to write about bullfighting. Ten thousand words they wanted, not really enough to do it justice, but that's not a fair excuse for not doing my job.

C: Ten thousand?

H: [mostly to self] Wasn't thinking straight when I took it on; never liked "writing to order." [back to C] They then said they'd take thirty or forty, but I ran to a hundred and twenty.

C: Thousand?

H: Couldn't get it down, even for a decent book. Hotch had to help me.

C: [statement, tired of asking questions] "Hotch."

H: Hotchener, a friend. Could have been anyone—anyone could have done it. I could have done it—always did, edit the shit out of everything—never got anything good until I'd rewritten it twenty times. [C stops self from saying "Twenty?"] Now, I couldn't make art out of a subject I know and love. When you can't write good about the things you enjoy ... You're stuck with a catalogue of the things you can't do anymore.

C: Not that we could always do everything. But when we got lost, we worked at it until we figured out something.

H: Or just worked at it, and worked some more.

C: Or realized we were trying too hard: relaxed, waited 'til it came right.

H: Waiting. That's one of the things I can't do. Good God, did I always have so little patience?

C: Probably. P'rhaps not. We're not as tall as we used to was.

H: No-o. So?

C: Joints shrink? vertebrae compress? Or it may be due to the circumstance that our tempers grow shorter.

H: Ha, I'll put that to the quacks next time I see them!

C: O.K. [chuckles] Meanwhile ... [drinks]

H: All of which, whatever that catalogue may be, with an ample supply of this, I can abide. [touches bottle but does not drink] The question is, if I have this in ample supply, can anyone abide me?

C: Oh you don't seem too ornery a character.

H: A "public face" I can put on. [a little agitated, mostly to self] Think I can fool the quacks, probably can't fool the G-Men. No, no, I'm hiding out here from the bio-grafters and professional critics. I still have enough contact with the good writers and publishers. I need to work hard for several hours every day, then I need congenial company, let the brain run an easier track.

NURSE: [from off stage left] Mr. Hemingway, ... ?

H: Yes.

NURSE: [entering] I'm looking—ah, Mr. Cobb.

C: Hello again.

NURSE: Hello. If you would be so good as to go down the hall to your left, to the Radiology Department, and introduce yourself to the receptionist, I believe they can take you directly.

C: [rises] Very well, thank you. [to H] Excuse me.

H: Come back if you can.

C: Alright. [Exit stage left.]

NURSE: Now, Mr. Hemingway, this is a bit embarrassing, but I'm afraid I have mislaid your medical file. I had it before the little disturbance here earlier, and afterwards I didn't. One possibility, therefore, is that I left it somewhere in here. Have you seen it?

H: Hmmm. What sort of information are we talking about, which has gone missing and floats about public, as well as private, halls and grounds?

NURSE: Umm, I wouldn't put it quite like that. I'm sure it's now in someone's possession. It is, of course, clearly labeled "confidential": your admission work-up, basic medical history, [hesitantly] some personal history, more detailed description of recent diagnoses—

H: Yes, well, I haven't left the room. Mr. Cobb you just saw, apparently empty-handed. That leaves you and Mort. Any chance Mort picked it up and returned it? He have access to filing departments and such?

NURSE: He does sometimes run errands to and from Central Records, and I suppose, on his own initiative—

H: Pretty resourceful little Man Friday.

NURSE: I'll check.

H: Of course, even if he took it back, Lord knows if he got it in its right place. Think he understands your filing system?

NURSE: As you say, Lord knows, but if he finds the proper area it will be simply alphabetical. Please ask him about it if you see him first.

H: Indeed, I will be happy to.

NURSE: Thank you. Good-bye then. [Exit stage left.]

H: Good-bye! [full breath] Possibilities begin to suggest themselves. [H rises and paces a bit.] Perhaps. [strides firmly to dresser, shuffles papers a bit placing one from middle on top, writes a line, poises pencil above page, as if to count words, but places in robe pocket]

MORT: [knocking stage right] Mr. H.

H: Yes, Mort, come ahead. [Mort enters carrying a baseball bat, thick-handled and shiny.] What have you there, my lad?

MORT: I want to ask Mr. Cobb to sign this [extending it to H].

H: [H tosses glasses on bed and takes bat, glancing at barrel as he moves his hands down to "wrap" the handle. He casts his hands and takes a muscle-bound swing.] Grrr.

C: [appearing stage left] Whoa, big guy, what are you trying to kill?

H: Some see windmills; I see Dodgers!

C: [entering] Shouldn't that be "Giants"?

H: And Pirates! [slashing as with a cutlass]

C: Alright, Wendy. How about Tigers?

MORT: And Indians!

H: [war whoops] And, most fearsome beasts of all, Senators. Washington!

C: First in war, first in peace,

BOTH: and last in the American League. [They laugh.]

H: The sh-stuff we remember.

MORT: [to C] I've got a bat for you.

H: Genuine Nellie Fox Major League model, good, solid, slap-hitter's plank, [paddling motion] keep your canoe moving when you go duck hunting.

[passes bat to C, who takes it in his fingers, keeping elbows in]

C: You pretty fast? [Mort smiles] Good choice then [tosses bat to Mort].

MORT: Oh, I'm not going to play with it anymore. [offers it back toward C]

C: Hold on, let's see if you know how to handle it. Mr. Hemingway obviously doesn't.

H: Hah!

C: Out in the fingers a bit, loosen up your hands, unlock your wrists, feel the control.

MORT: [moving bat with fingers and wrists] Hey!

C: Now, where's the label?

H: You should be able to read it.

MORT: [rotating bat] Oh, yeah.

C: Why's that? Bring the bat down to the hitting position, in front of the plate.

H: Label should be on top. Good. [C is moving Mort's top hand to place palm behind bat] Not so likely to break the bat when you hit that way.

C: Why's that?—let the kid answer.

MORT: Why does it help to not break the bat?

C: Right.

MORT: You don't want to hit the ball on the label. That's a weak spot.

C: No, you don't want the ball to hit the bat that close to the hands, but you avoid that by rotating the hips and shoulders, keeping your hands in until you get around. Why do you want the label up?—or down is equally good. [pause, Mort thinking] Your father probably knows.

MORT: Oh, he, uh—

C: Your grandfather certainly would have. Sixty years ago kids went out hunting, gathered wood, sawed and split it, whittled, built things—heck, maybe shaped their own bats. [grabs the bat and holds it up at Mort's eye level] Look at the side. What do you see? In the wood?

MORT: Lines.

H: The grain.

C: [turning bat so Mort can see other side] Layers of wood, going right through the bat, gives you a more solid hit if you line them up with the pitch. The label is always cut into the top layer. Find it, and you know how the grain goes. Probably guys in pro ball right now, know how to hit but don't understand the wood. [offers bat back, but Mort motions for him to keep it]

MORT: I'd like you to autograph it, please.

C: You want me to sign it? How do I write on a bat?

H: Oh, you carve "TC heart M"; it'll be fun; [partially opens drawer as if to find knife; leaves partially open] I'll help.

C: Eff off.

MORT: I'll get a pen; it'll leave a mark.

C: Get some sandpaper, if you can. Your bat has some kind of lacquer on it. We didn't varnish bats in my day. Boned 'm ...

[Mort looks startled/puzzled.]

H: Got a meat bone from the butcher, rubbed the bat with it, calcium supposed to harden the wood. [Mort turns to leave, stops to tidy bed.]

C: I'd use the bone to rub in tobacco so the juice would "set" the seams. One fella laid his in crankcase oil over winter. Those were probably hard to write on. [Mort finishes straightening H's bed; at some point he had put H's glasses in his pocket so he could use two hands to make a hospital corner and pat down the edges.] Hold on, get my pen, it's in my overcoat hanging by the front door.

MORT: Yes, sir.

C: And get something for Mr. Hemingway to sign. That'll impress the girls more.

MORT: Sure. [Exit stage right.]

H: Sure. [holds out hands for bat and takes it, moving it around in his fingers] Hmmm. So, a bit the professor yourself.

C: You know: those who can, do, those who can't, teach.

H: Oh yes, them that can't write—you know they have whole "courses" on it now, and yet about all you can pass on is "don't write too much or too fast." Anyway, they learn how to write by writing.

C: The knowledge is out there, if they pay attention. There was a few listened to me—Heilmann, Manush, Gehringer. [H nods impressed.] Players nowadays ... I think some of the Negroes have the talent and desire.

H: Robinson, Mays, Clemente.

C: Marvelous. Mays the only guy I'd pay to see today. And Jack. Helluva ballplayer. I still hold the record for stealing home; Robinson must have the most since the war. He had the fire and the fight. It was something to see when they let him loose.

H: [digging a little] Too bad the races were separated when you played.

C: Hmmm. I hadn't figured it that way. Maybe I could have worked with those boys. I seem to have more patience with kids now than I had with grown men back then; couldn't see why younger guys, still in their prime, weren't doing—didn't seem to want to do—things I could still do.

H: Didn't have "the fire and the fight"?

C: Dedication to the game and desire to be the best.

H: More than desire [c nods]—the disease of having to be the best.

C: Anyway, I see some kids on a dirt field, in that "godforsaken state" as you call it, and I give them a few tips. We all enjoy it. I heard you did the same on that commie island.

H: Oh, I organized them a bit, one of my compulsions, to organize: fishing trips, corrida parties—

C: Huh?

H:—duck hunts [leads a bird with the bat] ... if I could get out of here, I'd have you up to Idaho for what's left of the season.

C: Maybe another year. I've got a couple beautiful dogs you'd enjoy.

H: Yeah. Anyway, I gave them uniforms and equipment, but those kids had more natural talent—I couldn't give them many "tips." Might be able to help Mort a bit. Nice of you to treat him decent.

C: Does that boy actually do any work around here?

H: Oh, yes! Cleans a bit, ...

C: Pail not just a prop, then?

H: Perhaps. But my suspicion is he's part of the treatment program: distraction therapy.

C: Amusement therapy.

H: Fairly earns his wage entertaining us.

C: Or you him.

H: Or each the other. One of those whatchamacallit relationships.

C: "Symbiotic."

H: That's it, thanks. Damned drugs! I'd forget my name sometimes if I weren't so famous.

C: Same here: [raises flask but does not drink] the medicine.

H: Ah, no, alas, they don't dispense medicine here. Drugs, long chemical names, not short and sweet like "Jim" and "Johnny. Here, [reads pajamas cuff slowly:] methylphenidate: Ritalin.

C: Anti-de-pressant.

H: So they would have us believe.

C: I don't know if belief has anything to do with it, but I do believe I get the same results from Jack. [drinks]

H: Ha! you're not so dumb for a millionaire.

C: Your friend Fitzgerald's statement about the rich and us can't be taken too broadly. You see, I've read a little, even some of yours.

H: But more of my friend Fitzgerald's?

C: No, probably not. He was always a favorite with the ballplayers. You came a little after.

H: Ah, well, as you came a little before Ruth, in time, but ranked considerably behind him in popularity.

C: Now he was different from you and I. Certainly not brighter. Certainly very popular.

H: How did you feel about that? [tosses the bat to C and snaps his fingers at wing stage left, from which appears a psychiatrist's couch (strong legs with fixed {one directional} casters), which stops 10 feet or less from wing, pushed by Mort, a vision of a 1920's Viennese psychoanalyst, three-piece suit, reading glasses, a pad and ballpoint pen—beard and cigar optional]

C: How did you feel about Fitzgerald [sits on couch, points bat at H]?

DOCTOR MORT: [moves toward H, attempt at German accent] Tell me about yuh muttuh.

C: Tell us about your father. [holds nub of bat to side of head, "pulls trigger," rolls eyes up, tosses bat to H]

H: Tell us about your father and your mother. ["aims" at, "fires," and throws bat to C]

DrM: [Head has gone back and forth, trying to keep up, forgets German accent, to C:] What about your mother and your father?

PATIENT C: [reclining on couch, hugging bat] My father was a very strict man, towards me and towards his wife. He was a schoolteacher, a principal, "headmaster" you might say, and a county school commissioner. He made up the Latin name "Tyrus" after the city of Tyre; he admired the courage of its army in resisting Alexander the Great. Probably wanted to encourage me not to let anyone keep me down. Except himself. "Align yourself on the side of right and fear no man." He was the only person who could make me mind, and he always made me study. But scholarship was a field in which I knew I could never match him. Before he died he was also a newspaper publisher and a state senator.

[C stops; DrMort waits; H motions for "more"]

DrM: Venn did he die?

H: How did he die?

PATIENT C: I was away when he died. He'd have preferred I went to West Point, but a military life didn't seem an improvement on the bondage I felt at home, and I went off to play baseball. He told me not to come home if I didn't succeed in the profession. "Don't come home a failure." My mother was home alone when he died. The jury did not find against her.

[Mort looks even more puzzled; H looks skeptical.]

H: The Short Happy Life of William Herschel Cobb.

PATIENT C: I don't blame her for his death; I never blamed myself. I didn't need his ... help; he didn't need mine. I helped my mother when I made money in baseball and stocks. [Pause; again H motions for more.]

DrM: [German pronunciation] Alzo, als Kind: did you denn vant yuh fattuh tsu muhduh, und yuh muttuh tsu marry?

[H raises hand over face, may mutter nein, but as C rants looks with respect to DrM.]

PC: Hell no! I vanted to beat the shit out of anybody who stood in my path. It made me want never to finish second! [H half bows to Mort as C smiles, perfectly calm, rises, hands H bat, and pats him on shoulder.] You're up. Get down.

DrM: [still trying to keep up] Tell uz about yuh fattuh?

PATIENT H: [reclining on couch with bat] Like Cobb's, she was strict, "straight-laced," pious. Nobody smoked, drank, swore, or "fooled around" in our house; she was so afraid I'd get hurt somehow that she drove me straight to threat and danger. And her husband to suicide. We have never been friends—I hate her guts and she hates mine—although I try to support her. [pause]

C: Mother. Ask him about the Muttuh.

DrM: Alzo, tell uz about yuh muttuh.

PATIENT H: He was a country doctor, very dedicated, rode 'round to see his patients, many of whom couldn't pay him, or didn't because he didn't demand it. I'd come along sometimes, and he also took me hunting. [musing] He was as fast with an old lever-action Winchester as anyone I ever knew, with any kind of gun. [back] I learned about death on those jaunts, and a kind of courage in the face of grim reality, but not danger: he never shot at anything that could have fought back. He probably should have stood up to my father more; I wish he had. But instead he submitted to her and occasionally took it out on us children. A cowardly bully. And my other parent killed him as sure as Cobb's mother killed his father. It wasn't her finger which pulled the trigger, but it was out from under her thumb that he crawled to that place where it seemed to make sense to do it. [H stares off into distance.]

DrM: [uncertainly] Aber yuh muttuh—

PH: To be fair, he was suffering from real physical diseases: diabetes and hypertension and angina pectoris. Headaches and insomnia, could have been "home" grown or come from his financial problems. He crashed before the crash, lost a bundle on land in Florida in '27, held on to it when he should have sold. Impractical, indecisive, too cautious, a dreamer not a darer. But he gave me fishing, which is a pleasure to the end of your life, and I was fond as hell of him.

DrM: Alzo, did you denn vant yuh fattuh zu muhduh und … yuh … [realizes confusion, comes to a halt]

PATIENT H: Hell, no, I vanted liberty. It made me want no woman—mother, sister, wife, especially wife—to destroy my confidence or obstruct me from writing as well as I or anybody can write, or hold me back from anything I really cared about and couldn't imagine living without! [rises, tosses bat to C] Turn about. [C shoulders "rifle," he and H march to either side of Dr. Mort.] Pri-so-ner, mhaa!

[All march to stage right opposite couch, turn to face it. H takes Dr. Mort's pad and pen and puts them in his robe pocket; takes suit jacket and holds it open so Mort can place cigar and goatee, if Mort has them, in inside pocket; takes glasses, looks at them with some puzzlement, and puts them in his other robe pocket; places coat on couch and moves between and behind (upstage of) Mort & C, facing audience.]

H: Hey, batter, batter, batter.

[H touches ear, nose, thigh, chin, forearm; Mort touches two fingers to forehead; C assumes sacrifice-bunt stance with bat about belt level.]

H: Go! [Mort charges toward C and slides under bat. C spreads hands and bat in "safe" sign. H cheers:] Rah! Yea team! [Mort "doffs cap," takes off vest and lays it on couch. H pats Mort on fanny in direction of starting point.] Ninety feet from pay dirt.

[Mort walks back to his starting spot; C back in "batter's box" may mime spitting on hands, adjusting cup, knocking dirt off spikes, digging in, while Mort and H proceed.]

H: Now running for Bobo Newsom, number double zero, Dr. Death. [Mort shudders slightly but finishes stretching and deep breathing and turns to the center, as H sings:] "Our boys will shine tonight,

C: [sings] our boys will shine;

BOTH: Our boys will shine tonight, all down the line;

Our boys will shine tonight, our boys will shine;

H: When the sun goes down,

C: and the moon comes out,

BOTH: our boys will shine."

[H, behind C, toward Mort, touches left ear, forearm, thigh, draws finger across throat, holds hands up as though praying but pressing together with obvious force; Mort recoils slightly, somewhat hesitantly brings up two fingers to touch forehead.]

H: [leans towards C and stage-whispers:] Suicide squeeze.

C: [stage whisper:] Good call, skipper. [to Mort smartly touches forehead with two fingers (part baseball sign, part salute), resumes batting stance]

[Mort dashes towards C, C quickly lowers bat for "bunt," "takes a step towards first" (upstage) as Mort launches himself over bat and onto couch, which rolls into the wings. H & C cheer again. C stands "at ease" with bat.]

C: The battle o'er, the vict'ry won.

H: [takes out glasses and puts them on, carefully takes notebook and pen from other pocket] He's pretty good.

C: [taking pen from H] What?

H: Herr Doktor Wienerschnitzel.

C: Hmmph. He does charge a very fair hourly rate.

H: [reading] "Modest, diffident, humble, self-effacing, ..."

C: Let me have a sheet of that while you dream your analyses. [H dislodges and hands C a sheet.] Thanks.

H: "Kind, generous, loyal ..."

C: [pretends to read his sheet] "Obsessive, aggressive, depressive." [lightly rubs sheet over a small area of the bat]

H: [flips through "notebook," now clearly a packet of sandpaper] "Clear-sighted perceptions of self and others, well adjusted neurotic balance, compensating for physical debilities by reliance on scrambled intellects." [turns back to C and audience and tosses pad in "knife" drawer] Didn't you ever wish you were loved?

C: By whom?

H: [slowly shuts drawer, turns] Oh, you know, the whole world.

C: I was never a person of your scope. Breadth and depth.

H: You were a star. You were the best.

C: My "career" was much shorter than yours [finishes signature with a flourish].

H: There are toreadors in Spain, bullfighters,—

C: Little guys who flit around in tight pants and funny hats?

H:—guys who may start practicing at the age of five, hone their skills, refine their art for years, until they can hang within a silk thread of the horns, before the people even hear of them, who are adored.

C: Meanwhile another kid commences to practice.

H: Hundreds, if not thousands. And, yes, eventually the people adore one of them.

C: [tosses sandpaper in wastebasket] Well, the "national pastime."

H: You were on the national stage.

C: They gave you the "Ignoble Prize" in Sweden.

H: More people, of all ages, all classes, all levels of education, some who could not even read,—

C: Like the shoeless moron I had to fight for the batting title!

H:—others who could, but never read a novel in their lives,—

C: I always beat him.

H:—many more followed your game than took any notice of my art.

C: But predominately males. By a huge margin males. I'm not sure—

H: I'm not talking about that kind of "love."

C: Although there was that, too; probably also with the bullfighters.

H: Damn it! Can't you admit "respect" is lacking some fullness of feeling—

C: As you said, I was also hated.

H:—some dimension of warmth which could have radiated to the still pulsing core of your frozen, fossilized soul?

C: Hey!

H: [sits] Oh, I don't feel in possession of any nobler spirit. And, as you said, I pissed off my share, some of whom, at least now and then, I would rather had loved me.

C: It's natural.

H: Yes?

C: To want to be loved. It's a need.

H: Aha! [not so triumphant:] Also, a crazy, contrary need to hurt those we love, who love us.

C: They are the easiest.

MORT: [knocks off stage right] Mr. H?

H: Now what?

MORT: Is Mr. Cobb there, and can I come in?

H: Kids.

C: And dogs.

H: Most dogs. Yes, yes you may. [Mort enters.] The Peach has something for you.

MORT: [puzzled, but C extends bat] Oh, beautiful, thank you, Mr. Cobb. [Mort takes bat and props it against wall.] And, uh, we studied this last term.

H: [looks at book—beat—but does not take it] That's a good night-school read.

C: [takes book, reads cover] The Old Man ... and the Sea, ..

MORT: My teacher said, if I could get it autographed, ...

C: ... by Ernest Hemingway.

MORT: ... I could keep it.

[Mort & C look at H, two beats.]

H: 'tis a tale told by an Indian, full of sound and fury, signifying .. not a heckuva lot.

MORT: Oh, no, ...

H: No? The triumph of bone-headedness over inevitability? Doesn't happen; can't happen.

MORT: No, ... but ...

H: [sigh, as though resigned] I know: strong, brave, simple-, oops, pure-minded poor motherrr's son, master of his craft—if not his boat—

C:—which is more or less at the command of another master—

H:—in heroic struggle, outlasts mother nature and father time, and, making it all worth ... whatever it's worth, ends up ... where we all end up. [pause]

C: Extra innings, tie game, called for darkness. Here, you can use my pen.

H: To be completed at a later date: tomorrow, and tomorrow, ... [pause]

MORT: But, it's beautifully written.

H: It's a masterpiece; everyone knows that! [takes pen and book and signs] I got the Pulitzer for it, and a loada money. [holds up book]

MORT: [takes book carefully, and C takes pen] Then ... ?

H: Then ...now ... I don't know. As the old Indian said—a different one: long-ago time, good; now, heap shit.

[Pause, H and Mort both defeated.]

C: Go on, show it to Mary.

MORT: Oh, I don't know.

C: Nobody knows around here. Not that I'm sure I want to know …

H: Indeed, mostly grim.

C: Mostly? You're cracked; I'm dying.

H: That's the story in brief. The catastrophe's in the details.

C: Uh-huh, which they don't know or don't tell us. Well, maybe it's time—time to break up the party.

H: I can see the hilarity is making Mort a little light-headed.

C: I'll go try to find out something about what's left of my prostate. Don't get up to too much fun while I'm gone. [Exit stage right.]

MORT: Good luck, Mr. Cobb. [two beats] Is he really dying?

H: We all are. [hopeful shift to reassure Mort] Of course I don't know. Nor does he. Which reminds me, Mort. [H goes to dresser] There's been a mistake—not yours. Mr. Cobb asked to have his file brought here, but they delivered mine instead. [file from bottom drawer] Could you take this, without reading it—[stage whispers as points to word on cover, handing file to Mort] "confidential"—and bring back Mr. Cobb's? You know where the files are?

MORT: [puts file under his orderly's jacket] Sure, Records Room, everything's there.

H: Excellent. Don't let them give you any trouble—"you're not authorized," b-s like that. If they won't give you Mr. Cobb's file, explain the mix-up, and don't give them mine until they give you his.

MORT: O.K. They know me there. I can handle it myself.

H: Even better, always the best way. Here, [holds out silver dollar; Mort raises hand, doesn't want to take money] from Mr. Cobb, brought from "the Silver State," a lucky charm for the "quest."

MORT: Yes, sir, thanks, Mr. H. [pockets silver dollar] And thanks for the autograph. Wow, a bat and a book. [picks up bat and exits stage right]

H: A bell and a candle. Out, out ... Well, we get up to what we can. Come on, Papa. Just a quick one. [drinks] And then we'll see what the Clinic knows about Mr. Tyrus R. Cobb. [sighs, sits] Hell, one more [drink]. [rises again, nervous, moves toward bed but turns back to dresser, rearranges papers, looks at top sheet, looks back at bed, takes pencil and writes a sentence, looks at it with pencil poised then marks a period] [vague PA message stage right; knock] Come.

MORT: [entering stage right] Here it is.

H: And nobody saw you—still a surprise?

MORT: I saw Mr. Cobb as I left here, but he didn't see your file. I distracted him with the bat and the book [hands file, which will be a different color from the one he took, to H].

H: I'm not sure I even want to try to picture that.

MORT: Oh, I just told him thank you again and that I was going to put them in my safe place. And I did, but I put your file back in Central Records and took out Mr. Cobb's. Nobody saw anything. Now I better get back so they don't miss me.

H: Right-o. Thanks, Mort.

MORT: [exiting] You're welcome, Mr. H.

H: [opens file on dresser top] "December 18, 1886." Oh, yeah, still fighting the Civil War. "Estimated ..." [flips back to cover] Damn fool kid. Interesting, however ... not only that the hospital has a complete filing system for donors, or potential donors, but that Cobb's file is this thick. [leafing through fairly rapidly, muttering:] "Memorial Hospital ... Educational Foundation" ... college scholarships ... pensions ... ballplayers without pensions ... look at that, they've got numbers. "Babe Ruth Charity Golf Tournament": one of those war-bonds things? [Knocking stage right; H quickly places file under papers.] Come.

C: [enters with three split pieces of wood and a Wall Street Journal] Oh. Writing?

H: No. Yes. One line. Not any more. Come on, come on in.

C: Alright. Pull up a chair. [approaches stove; as H pulls the smaller chair to stove and sits, C crumples piece of paper and hands to H.]

H: Stock listings?

C: [places rest of paper in wastebasket] I take care of that first thing every day.

H: Hmmm. [placing paper in stove] If you dabble in commodities, I've got some old manuscripts the professors seem to think might make good investments.

C: I'm sure they would, assuming I outlived you, which is unlikely.

H: [taking wood] Where did you find these?

[As they talk, H loads the three pieces of wood; C sits on bed, which is close to stove.]

C: Took a walk 'round the castle. They've got a nice woodpile—maybe an old boiler somewhere.

H: For emergency. Obviously don't feed these anymore.

C: Clean?

H: Yup. Still, almost winter now—[Conversation continues as Nurse enters stage left, dressed as early 20th-century country-store clerk, apron, perhaps straw hat, tossing an apple to H, one to C, who start eating. Nurse kneels before stove; movements indicate she is striking match and holding it to newspaper. Shuts stove door (there may be a red light in stove) and exits stage right.]

C:—time for the hot-stove league.

H: I still follow the game. New York's not my favorite city, but a good place to watch the Series. Couldn't make it this year, but heard reports: another seven-game classic.

C: 1960, Bill Mazeroski. I guess that won't be hard to remember.

H: [mostly to himself] Remembrance, anticipation of the renewed conflict; tempts one to believe life's worth a shit. [beat] Hard to keep up these days—they have a team up here now!

C: Teams moving around, managers moving around. Too many trades, even interleague. Still winter's pretty much the same. Chance for every fan to think his team could finish first next season. The triumph of hope over experience.

H: Every player going to have a better year. Except they won't. And the game changes, but it doesn't.

C: Like most things.

H: Plus ca change, plus ca reste meme. Old men, sitting around the fire, talking about the past. I suppose everybody asks you to compare your day to the present.

C: Today's much easier for hitters. Became so to some extent in my time: spitter, shine ball, emery ball, every kind of freak ball outlawed; lively ball.

H: But they play, what, almost half the games at night now?

C: I don't think that's a great handicap to the hitters, and consider this: they bring in a bright new ball forty times a game. We had to hit against the same ball which may have been hit into the stands and thrown back a dozen times, cut, sanded, spat on, and the saliva colored by the tobacco, slippery elm, or licorice chewed to produce it, until it was darker than a club owner's heart. Today's game is much tougher for pitchers; pitchers not so tough.

H: There's a few teams have a good tandem. Spahn-Burdette. Drysdale-Koufax.

C: The Indians had a bunch of good righties after Feller: Lemon, Wynn, Garcia. And Herb Score, a great lefty.

H: Doesn't look like Score's coming back.

C: If he doesn't, he's got to move on, as do we all. It'll be some time before we see his equal. They're adding major league teams, losing farm teams. More kids going to college, wrecking their arms before they get started, less kids playing sandlot.

H: Less sandlots. What do you think you'd hit against today's pitchers?

C: Around the league average: two-sixty in the NL last year?

[Mort appears with his pail stage right, but, seeing H and C talking, stands quietly.]

H: Two-sixty? You hit .367 against Walter Johnson, Herb Pennock, ... Cy

Young for Chrissake.

C: Rube Waddell, Ed Walsh, [here and at other breaks, a bite of apple]—

H: Old spitballer, known in Chicago as the only man who could strut sitting down.

C:—Smokey Joe Wood ...

H: Three-Finger Brown, Carl Mays [apple—Mort reacts, leaves.] Babe Ruth.

C: Didn't hit .367 against Ruth. Son-of-a-bitch was a tough lefty. I managed about .325, by choking up, bearing down—

H: When were you not bearing down?

C: punching singles to left. Very few righthanded batters touched him for extra bases. I believe he could have been one of the all-time greats as a pitcher if he hadn't turned to slugging, but that role was probably a better fit with his intemperate lifestyle.

H: O.K., Ruth, Walsh, etc., .325, but against the whole NL today, Spahn, Drysdale, and all the third, fourth, fifth starters, around .260?!

C: You have to remember, I'm 73 years old.

H: Ha!

C: In 1927, when I was 40, I hit .357. Few cared; Ruth hit 60 home runs, and, to give him credit, averaged .356.

H: Son-of-a-bitch could hit.

C: No question. Next year, 1928, the league average was .280. I hit .323. So did Ruth, but he hit 54 homers.

H: An off year.

C: I hung 'em up. I had beat myself up so much over the years, taking chances, that I couldn't afford anymore to take chances—which you have to do, have to be aggressive on the ballfield—and I'd long been making more money with investments than from my baseball salary: an easy choice.

H: Not an easy decision at all. Many continue 'til they fall well below that level of excellence.

C: Excellence! They say baseball's the only field of endeavor where you can fail two-thirds of the time and still be a hero.

H: Oh, no. I write three stories, two go straight in there [fire]. If the third turns out good I keep writing. Still, "hero" is a relative term. And then there's "idol." And "beloved idol."

C: Eh?

H: It must have been something else to be "The Bambino."

C: Huh! "The Sultan of Swat."

H: [rising] You work your butt off to be regarded as first in your field, and along comes this character [flips apple core in wastebasket]—well, if anyone was ever "bigger than life." [As he talks, addressing an imaginary "audience," H takes a large camel-hair overcoat from the wardrobe, puts it on, a "driver's"(?) cap, puts it on, pulls a cigar out of one of the coat's pockets.] "He was a circus, a play, and a movie all rolled into one. Kids adored him, women loved him, men idolized him. There was something about him that made him great." [Lefty Gomez]

C: Oh, he was a goddam carnival, fun and excitement for all, every ride running at full speed. If he'd been human, like the rest of us, like your friend Fitzgerald [apple]—.

H:—the crack-up would have been awesome and sickening. But he played for twenty-two years and lived ten years longer than Fitzgerald. In spite of all the appetites—cigars, booze, women, big meals and big spending—

C: Everyone in the American League cherished the hope that the Big Guy would eat and drink himself into a stupor and be unable to get the bat around his stomach, but it was the falsest of dreams.

H:—in spite of all, he did, and made it look effortless, what everyone after him has labored to do. Not merely with power, but with skill and grace, he dominated the game and changed the game.

C: There was no strategy—[rises] no scheming and craftiness—[hurls core into basket] no game.

H: There was excitement, drama. [as Ruth] "I swing big, with everything I've got. I hit big or I miss big. I like to live as big as I can."

C: He came up to the plate and went back to the dugout, one way or the other; that was all the "drama" there was!

H: He was the god who circled the bases, as the sun circles the earth—

C: [through clenched teeth] No-it-doesn't.

H: and we cheered him, and his glory warmed and cheered us. And he was the god who died and went under the ground—

C: Ohhhh, horsefeathers!

H: sputter, sputter—and our hopes died with him, and we mourned, and rejoiced when he came up again to continue the cycle.

C: [very close to H] In 1936, who got the most votes?

H: Ty Cobb.

C: More than everybody's favorite Babe, [snatches cigar, stuffs it back in Ruth's coat pocket] more than Dutch Wagner, [H takes pipe out of other pocket.] Walter Johnson, Christy Matthewson: also beloved ballplayers.

H: [academic, gestures with pipe] Because, on the field, in the words of Professor Tristram Speaker, "The Babe was a great ballplayer, sure, but Cobb was even greater. Ruth could knock your brains out, but Cobb would drive you crazy."

C: A well qualified judge, perhaps biased by friendship. Oh, yes, I had friends.

H: But love isn't a judgment.

C: No.

H: Not bestowed grudgingly. Though the grudge, contrariwise to the friendship, may add authority to the judgment: ["gravelly" Ruth voice] "Cobb is a prick. But he sure can hit. God Almighty, that man can hit."

C: George Herman himself.

H: [musing to self] After Italy trip, studied life of Dante—seemed to be one of worst jerks who ever lived, but how well he could write! This may be a lesson to us.

JIMMY CANNON MORT: [enters stage left, talking as he walks across behind H&C, reporter's hat, pen, striped shirt, suspenders] "He was the strangest of all our national sports idols. But not even his disagreeable character could destroy the image of his greatness as a ballplayer. [stops walking] Ty Cobb was the best. [exiting stage right] That seemed to be all he wanted."

H: [nodding towards Mort's exit] Drank with that guy in New York, Jimmy Cannon. Had a beautiful ear, when not drunk, and great reportorial integrity.

C: Like Hemingstein, better when used short words.

H: Off-field the Bambino was the crazy one, like his Roaring Twenties: everyone's friend, careless and tireless. At every small burgh he came to he hit the longest ball ever seen in them parts and then visited kids at the local hospital.

C: But never built one.

H: But Cobb's private life was private, plodding, hunting through winter in your weighted boots to keep your legs strong, careful, circumspect, as though you wished to live forever.

C: And here we still are. [As H proceeds, C takes tie from wardrobe, ties it, vest, puts it on but does not button up.]

H: A piece of us. But every spring, long after the dead ball era had been exploded by the Babe, you stormed back onto the field, running into walls and over infielders, as though it was your last day, working pitchers for bases on balls, bunting and stealing [still waving pipe] and fighting your own pre-world-war-one hand-to-hand conflict of attrition, to see who would surrender first, the opposition on the field or the poor, bewildered fanatics in the grandstands. [C snatches pipe and puts it in his back pocket.]

C: And, in between the macho episodes of your unprivate life, living yourself as though there was no tomorrow, or as though you didn't care how or when you died, while Fitzgerald caught the wild and sophisticated spirit of the urban age, you were writing your meticulous little stories about hunters and boxers, foreign wars and drunken tourists, bullfighters and ... friggin' fishermen.

H: Cobb went to a ballgame, and war broke out.

C: The Great American Game should be an unrelenting war of nerves.

H: Hemingstein went to a war, and literature broke out.

C: But Fitzgerald exploited the zeitgeist—

H: Oooh!

C: [takes pipe out of back pocket] the spirit of his Roaring Twenties, the Country's Jazz Age—nightclubs and speakeasies, bathtub gin, big bands, fast dances, model T and bigger automobiles, easy money, lavish living—the decade of the $5 work day, the first transatlantic flight, and the movie star.

H: Was he a writer for all time, or just his age? Clown was hardly dead before he was anthologized and canonized.

C: And the subject of serious scholarly biographies. But let's not get ahead of ourselves: throughout his life he could sell anything he wrote.

H: He could have written less and much better.

C: He was welcomed in Hollywood.

H: Where character is perverted, art debased.

SHARED ASIDE:

C: Your books survived the silver screen. I wouldn't mind being debased by Ingrid Bergman.

H: I learned from Fitz and Faulkner. The only way to deal with Hollywood, you stand on the border of the next state and toss over the story after they hand you the suitcase of money.

C: [back to declaiming for the "symposium"] While others ground it out syllable by syllable, he produced elegant writing seemingly without effort.

H: Oh, the good stuff always takes effort; even for him the beautiful writing came through much labor—especially for him, married as he was to an extravagant nutcase, the fourteen-carat bitch.

C: Talk about "grace under pressure."

H: [beat] Hmmm ... [back to train of thought] He is the great tragedy of talent in our bloody generation. Scott took literature so solemnly. He never understood that it was just writing as well as you can and finishing what you start. Il faut d'abord durer.

C: [to imaginary audience] That is French, boys and girls, for "don't throw your arm out in the early innings." Remember you have to work steadily and consistently, probably four times through the lineup, in order to finish the game.

H: You write first for yourself, to make it as real and perfect as you can, and then for anyone you love. Scott, in his strange mixed-up Irish-Catholic monogamy, wrote for Zelda, and when he lost hope in her and she destroyed his confidence in himself, he was through. It was as though he had made his god a canoe, say, or anything that will not last, instead of a good graven image.

C: [aside to imaginary audience] Hold on tight, class, here comes the "my God" speech. [puts pipe in pocket]

H: My God painted many wonderful pictures and wrote some very good books and fought Napoleon's rear-guard actions in the retreat from Moskova and fought on both sides at Gettysburg, and killed George Armstrong Custer and did away with yellow fever, and taught Picasso how to draw and sired Citation. And my God when he played football was Jim Thorpe, and when he pitched he was Walter Johnson, [slower, again shared with C more than "audience"] and the ball looked as big as a small marble, and it would kill you if it hit you. So my God never dusted anybody off ever. [C nods; H acknowledges.] And, verily, if you were man enough to crowd the plate on him, my God, not wishing the death of even a shit or a prick, might take a little off his fastball, so you had a prayer of touching him for a bingle, or give you that day your base on balls.

BOTH: Amen.

H: [back] And the reason Zelda ruined Scott was that she was crazy, insanely jealous of his work and whenever he got going good would try to bust it up, and this wasn't difficult because he was a much more than potential rummy. What saved him was that he couldn't drink and would pass out cold at the number of drinks that would just make you and me feel good. Above all he was completely undisciplined and would quit at the drop of a hat and borrow someone's hat to drop. Zelda told him he was inadequate as a lover and his equipment too small, and he had seized on this as another excuse for defeat and would not be dissuaded, even though I took him into the john and show—

C: Thank you, Dr. Hemingstein. [leads gentle applause—takes out pipe, aside to "audience":] The trouble with the Germans is they don't have a word for Schadenfreude. [to H] When Fitzgerald "cracked," he admitted it.

H: Couldn't hide it so couldn't deny it.

C: And claimed that you cracked also, the difference being, quote, "his inclination is towards megalomania and mine toward melancholy."

H: Ah, alliteration, the elegant assonance and consonance and graceful balance. So refined. My expression was always a little rougher, elemental.

C: Fitzgerald's "melancholy," Hemingstein's "black ass."

H: [to self] Only beginning to feel it when Scott was struggling, so thought I was different. Didn't understand it at all when my father ... [to

C] And he had another lovely phrase: "In the real dark night of the soul it is always three o'clock in the morning."

[two beats—for both, too close to home]

"There are no second acts in American lives." I believe he was right.

C: [aside] God speed, young Mr. Score.

H: The laws of prose writing are as immutable as those of flight, of mathematics, of physics. Scott was almost completely uneducated. He knew none of the laws. He did everything wrong; and it came out right.

C: Baseball as Ruth reinvented it is geometry and physics—[aside] ninety percent of my success was psychological, but now, as our contemporary philosopher puts it, "fifty percent of the game is half mental." [back] The big monkey inherited the craft of the old game, and he was strong as hell, though I couldn't see he ever did much to get or stay that way, seemed to do everything to ruin his physical constitution, and only had one good eye—

H: Right. Same here.

C:—but he had extraordinary timing.

H: But geometry always catches up with you.

[C and H begin musing separately from each other and "audience."]

C: He was the most unaffected and natural man I ever knew, a great inspiration to all the youngsters of America, which I always admired. It's staggering to think what he might have done with his marvelous ability if he'd had a little self-control.

H: A year before he "crashed" he finished Tender is the Night, and it's amazing how excellent much of it is.

C: On what you would think was his worst day, he'd show up right about game time—hung over, queasy stomach—saying, "give me a bi"—

H: Much of that novel was so good it was frightening. If he had integrated it better ...

C: bicarbonate of soda—

H: as is, much of it is better than anything else he ever wrote.

C: haul himself up the dugout steps, weave his way to the plate, flick the goddam ball over the fence ...

H: At the same time churning out Hollywood hack work and pulp for the magazines.

C: and then trot around the bases with those tiny steps so he didn't tip over.

H: He may have wasted more talent than the rest of us had, singly or all together.

C: Guys he played against said "he ain't human." The record supports that.

[H&C come together.] You drive yourself,

H: You work like hell,

C: study every aspect of the game,

H: keep writing until you get an understanding and a feel for your craft,

C: analyze your opponents, adapt your strategy, fight,

H: take on the great writers one by one until you match them,

C: [They are now looking at each other.] harness your powers, stick to the rules,

H: make up your own rules, bind yourself to them,

C: get in shape, stay in shape,

H: maintain the standards, discipline,

C: self-control, austerity.

H: speak for yourself. And at the same time there exists this ... undisciplined

C: undisciplined

H: extravagant

C: dissolute

H: self-indulgent, disgustingly,

C: unworthily,

BOTH: incredibly talented ...

[H&C take pipe and cigar from each other and clamp them fiercely in their teeth

[An intermission may be taken, if desired.]

as Mort enters stage right.]

MORT: Mr. H, what are you doing, it's too hot for that in here! [As H&C take off Ruth and Fitzgerald clothes—may dispose of pipe and cigar now or later—Mort opens stove door, shielding it from audience view, and mimes poking "fire," shuts door and takes H&C's clothes and puts them in wardrobe, as C notices window.]

C: Didn't see how big the woods was when I drove up here. Nice to get back to the Midwest. Few and different trees in the Silver State. Something about a good old forest. You go in, and it's what it is; what you're hunting is in there. You come out with it or not.

H: The trophy and the danger.

MORT: [closes wardrobe and turns to H&C] What did I come in here for? Oh, yeah. There's lunch. You can go to the cafeteria, or I can bring you a tray.

C: No, thanks, we've eaten.

MORT: But, where—?

H: You'll find the remains [points to wastebasket].

MORT: Oh.

C: Maybe something more later.

MORT: O.K., I'll be back later. [Exit stage right.]

H: Right. Where were we?

C: In the woods?

H: I've been in some—one hellish forest in '44— always made it out. It's like I don't have the lore of this woods, can't read it, can't get through and come onto the clear, high ground ... by skill or luck.

C: Luck?

H: Luck, you old ballplayer. [During this long "luck" scene, off and on, H rubs his rabbit's foot and chestnut and a shiny pebble.]

C: All I know about "luck" I hear on the radio when I'm driving: in the country-western songs it rhymes with "pickup truck." If you buy a GM, my stock goes up, and you can rely on the pickup truck. You can also rely on observation and analysis; but a good batter never guesses with a pitcher.

H: I guess I've used up my guesses, too. What's the next level? ... "favored of the gods"?

C: Is that your religion?

H: Religion is superstition ... I believe in superstition.

C: Plenty of that among ballplayers, though I don't recall often hearing "favored of the gods."

H: At least not cursed.

C: Curses is psychology. I believe in psychology. I warded off the evil eye by being more evil myself.

H: Filed your spikes in plain view on the dugout steps.

C: Ah, I know people believe that, and I took the benefit of the misconception, but it never happened. Among other things.

H: Ha! Maybe you should write a book. [C nods.] I keep writing, trying for something better than I can do, but I've lost my craft.

C: Fear of failure? Come on, you've "made it." [H shakes head.] You can "retire at the top."

H: Very hard for a writer. People think, if you could ever do it you can always do it. A boxer or ballplayer, his legs go, he hangs up his shoes; everyone understands.

C: Except the player. He always reads about it in the paper before he admits it: [hand sweeps across headline] "Rivera's legs have gone."

H: Oh, yeah. "Jungle Jim."

C: Three years later, he retires. But say you're a hurler, lose command of your pitches, which are your tools—

H: Like recall and invention for a writer.

C: no one understands that.

H: Uh-huh.

C: You struggle for a couple more years, can't get it back, still no one understands, but you retire.

H: Then I'm no longer me.

C: I can never remember, is that "pride" or "vanity"?

H: Hubris: the young man's inheritance.

C: Stubbornness, inflexibility?

H: [more fiercely] The old man's prerogative.

C: Well, the old man's inheritance ...

H: No! It's terrible, terrifying, I can't stand it: I refuse.

C: Refuse? It's not a legal bequest or a writers prize you can turn down.

H: I defy them. The gods, the fates ... the Feds [shudders].

C: Windmill country again.

[beat]

H: Never-never land. ... I'm afraid ... that I, and whatever help—at least a faithful, if simple-minded, squire—between us, our two half wits, we don't have the arms.

C: I'd say that's a reasonable fear.

H: And let's also say, at the moment I have a problem with reason. Some "facts" I'd rather not face.

C: That may not be unreasonable. As Leo Durocher said, realists finish last.

H: Uh huh [affirmative]. "No horse named Morbid ever won a race."

C: In a losing race, somehow a man gets an edge, a shot in the arm in the dark, a groundless confidence that gives him the spirit to fight harder than he knows how to fight. Maybe the rabbit's foot. Or a faithful half-wit—[snaps fingers toward stage left] The old New York Giants had a mascot—[Mort as professor/don enters (pushing a chalkboard on wheels if it is not possible to drop one from above stage, see below), vest and pants from suit but no glasses, goatee, or cigar; English accent optional; H and C sit.]—he warmed up in the bullpen every game, thinking they might actually put him in; they won twenty-six in a row!

PROFESSOR MORT: [slightly pacing] What you refer to as "luck" is a normal phenomenon, capable of scientific study and measurement within the laws of statistics and probability. We say we "run out of luck," "have bad luck," or "something goes wrong" when, despite the probabilities being even, or in favor of something good, the bad thing happens.

H: Clear as mud.

P MORT: Simply put, "good luck" is beating the odds. [towards H] Should we say you are, for instance, lucky to be alive? [H glares at Mort.] According to the most recent actuarial tables utilized at this and other prestigious institutions in the continental United States, the life expectancy at birth of a white male is 67.4 years, [aside] as opposed to 60.7 for a Negro. So no, you are not "lucky," you have not beaten the odds. However, the odds of a passenger surviving the crash of a one- or two-engine small plane, twice, are slightly less than two to one against. So, yes, we should say you were lucky to be alive. However, passengers who were under the influence of alcohol at the time of a crash have three times the chance of avoiding separations, dislocations, compound fractures, severe shock, and attendant affects ...

C: [to H—simultaneously, Mort looks to the roof and snaps fingers, and a chalkboard descends (if possible)] Is that true?

H: I was relaxed. The pilot may have been potted. He was never tested.

C: No, I mean true about intoxication avoiding fractures and so forth.

H: Dunno. Too drunk to notice [smiles].

[Whenever the board stops in place, Mort pulls a piece of chalk from behind his ear and starts graphs, etc.]

C: If that worked on the ballfield, Ruth would have been a case study.

P MORT: ... [looking back to C&H] as opposed to those who were sober. To be absolutely accurate we require factors of speed, [frantic slashing of chalk on board] structure, altitude, angle of impact, composition of terrain—in the end, the odds appear neither heavily against you nor strongly in your favor. Ergo, therefore, no, we should not say you are lucky to be alive. [sticks chalk behind ear] Nor that you are unlucky.

H: Aarrgh. What about three European wars, many weeks at the front?!

P MORT: As an American, statistically, …

H: And several hours in the air.

P MORT: those experiences are not significant.

H: What?!

P MORT: As far as the odds of your now being alive, or not.

H: Or partially.

C: You could write a story, hero based on you! Title: "A Half-Slain Knight."

P MORT: Now, as to the interesting question of whether ritualistic behavior—superstitious practices—have any influence on the operation of the odds—and I say "interesting" not as it's being so inherently, as a serious hypothesis, but interesting in the fact that it is almost universally not a question: there seeming to be only the two camps, committed believers and confirmed skeptics. [spits on hands and rubs them together rapidly]

H: I wonder how this is going to come out.

C: Inconclusively, I would guess.

P MORT: Unfortunately, the scientific community being firmly established in the camp of doubters, there have been, as I implied, few rigorous tests of the hypothesis itself.

C: Ah-ha.

P MORT: What "evidence" we have offers no support for the efficacy of such observances. The odds—probabilities—do not seem to be changed. If, what seems, an unusually extended string of successes, uninterrupted by incidents of failure, such as returning with a large fish on each of six consecutive sailings, is temporally coextensive with a stretch of laundry laxity, such as not changing your underpants, that is indeed only a coincidence, easily within the laws of probability in conformance with ascertainable physical conditions, many of them, in this instance, seasonal.

H: Yeah, yeah, trade winds, moons.

C: Moons? Fish are lunatics?

P MORT: Saltwater fish.

H: Marlin run on the waxing moon. Current drops off in declining moon, fish won't eat. But during the running—

P MORT: The so-called token, charm, talisman, or—

C: Friggin' rabbit's foot.

P MORT:—operates, outside of a scientifically evolved culture, similarly to ritual observances intended to propitiate gods thought to punish neglect of such observances by plague, famine, war—

H: The Four Horsemen of the Apocalypse.

C: Death and taxes. [Mort & H disturbed]

P MORT:—where failure to discharge the conventional, ritualistic obligations may result in fines or imprisonment. [H more disturbed; C & Mort stare, puzzled at how they arrived here.]

P MORT: Only in the minds of the deluded. [snapping out of it] What does operate is natural law, cause and effect, rationally explicable, scientifically calculable.

C: So it's all probabilities.

H: And chance.

P MORT: Within the entire range of possibilities.

C: And that means—

H:—as surely as for the Ancients the Fates controlled—

C:—natural laws limit us.

P MORT: 'tis not destiny, but chemistry—

C: That sounds like a slogan DuPont rejected.

P MORT:—and physics.

[Mort snaps fingers and stops satisfied as chalkboard rises out of sight.]

H: So ... that's ... the fear. We're in this alone. Nothing, no one, helping.

C: Nor against us.

H: [gesturing at PM] And modern science tells us ...

P MORT: You collect the data, I calculate.

H: And conclude!

P MORT: No.

H: Advise ...

P MORT: Advice is not my department. You may draw your own conclusions, or, perhaps one of my colleagues may advise ...

H: Aarrgh! [snaps fingers and Nurse enters stage right, carrying small tray of medicine, as Mort exits stage left.]

NURSE: Gentlemen.

C: Nurse.

H: Are we doomed?

NURSE: [businesslike] That's an unusual way of putting it. [beat, answers] We have to [half smile] take our medicine. [Nurse places tray on dresser but hands H a blue bottle]

H: [relaxing a little] Ah, you Norveygians have such a madcap approach to life.

C: I think I'll go let the doctors collect some more data.

NURSE: This way, Mr. Cobb,—

C: Yes, Ma'am. [C starts off stage left.]

NURSE:—they'll be ready for you in Laboratory B.

H: [noticing C, behind Nurse's back, remove flask from pocket] Good luck with the medicine. [drinks his milk of magnesia]

C & NURSE: Tests. [C exits raising flask.]

H: [rises if still on bed] Now, about the medicine.

NURSE: Yes, I'm glad we're alone.

H: Oh?

NURSE: I believe you have a procedure tentatively scheduled? The doctors have described another course of treatment, if the drugs did not prove efficacious ... ?

H: Which I don't see that they have done.

NURSE: You're still up and down.

H: More often down, though perhaps not always as low.

NURSE: So this alternative treatment—

H: Run electricity through my skull,—

NURSE: Uh, basically—

H: reverse the polarities of my brain cells.

NURSE: I doubt that is how—

H: they would put it. No, and they won't say it's a CIA mind-control experiment, either!

NURSE: Certainly not.

H: [muttering to self] Liars, damned liars, and federal agents.

NURSE: Well, they would like another opportunity to explain and assist in your evaluation and decision.

H: Damned veterinaries. I would like to hear a more human view, yours for example.

NURSE: That would be far beyond my qualifications.

H: Not that I've seen.

NURSE: The doctors understand and can explain—

H: I want your understanding.

NURSE: It's quite technical. The scientific principles, underlying theory—

H: Stuff that.

NURSE: In fact, I'd say it is somewhat theoretical.

H: You'd say! Aha. That's what I want. That's all I want. What would you say about this other "theoretical" treatment?

NURSE: As I said, the doctors are very eager ...

H: I'll ... give odds they are. But you, don't you give me the royal, scientific runaround. Professor Slide Rule has just carried out one of the most masterful evasive maneuvers of modern military bullshitting. If I want the technical jibberjabber I'll hie me to the doctors. You can give me the true gen.

NURSE: The ... ?

H: "Gen," RAF slang for "intelligence," the briefing, what the brass tell the crews. The "true gen," very difficult, but absolutely essential to obtain, is what they know but don't tell you. ... Please.

NURSE: [quietly] As you know from their discussions, the other treatment is ... a bit—

H: Hellish?

NURSE: Not necessarily.

H: You mean you don't know?

NURSE: Drastic.

H: Necessarily?

NURSE: No, we cannot tell, from case to case, as with the medicine,—

H: Well, I think I can tell you about that.

NURSE: before the application, what, precisely, will be the results. For some subjects it does clear, invigorate the mind, so much so that, as with some drugs, one can become addicted.

H: Not I, won't be addicted, never been addicted to anything, except work, writing, the best drug.

NURSE: Everyone—almost everyone, with rare exceptions—thinks he is a special case.

H: [thinking out loud] Do remember after one of the times I got my arm crushed or shoulder twisted or some terribly painful smashup, they were afraid I'd get addicted and took me off the drug after five days. Believe I could easily have become a dopehead if it didn't constipate me.

NURSE: That does not appear to be one of the drawbacks of this treatment.

H: Constipation?

NURSE: Nor, usually, addiction. But there are no certainties: perhaps relief or improvement—possibly increased debilities.

H: But you do know ...

NURSE: We know there will probably be some short-term-memory loss, probably temporary. Some loss of long-term memory is possible ... headaches ...

H: From case to case.

NURSE: It's a decision the patient has to make. If you feel disinclined to continue with the medicine, well, that's your decision.

H: That's it.

NURSE: If so ...

H: That's what I thought. Sometimes I feel this, sometimes that, "disinclined" being the general attitude. My decision. Not too confident of that, or anything, these days. Easiest might be to get it over with. That might be my inclination.

NURSE: It is up to you.

H: [mutters] Up mine, any way I play it. [snaps fingers, as frustrated]

NURSE: Oh dear, [moves to exit] I'll try to find a fly swatter.

H: No, no, please stay here. [grabs snapping hand with other as Nurse turns back] Godammit. I need help, and I hate needing help. Shit!

NURSE: Ah, ..

H: Sorry. How do you swear?

NURSE: I can't.

H: Oh, hell, Nurse ...? [Nurse has crossed her arms so they and/or sweater cover name tag; H gestures to "open up."] Nurse ... Barkley. You're shitting me.

NURSE: My mother's name.

H: Goddammit, you ought to be able to swear. You know the words.

NURSE: No.

H: Yes. Probably even the French: Merde! German, Scheisse! Norveygian, Dritt!

NURSE: Oh, hell.

H: Yes. That's where I am. That's where you'll be some day. It gets worse—worst at the end, but it starts early. Here's two of us lost our fathers violently.

NURSE: Three.

H: Mort?

NURSE: Four.

H: You?

NURSE: That's not relevant.

H: You mean it's none of my business.

NURSE: No.

H: "No"?

NURSE: Yes, "no." "None."

H: O.K. My father was a coward, Cobb's a bully; still it's a wound. They loved us in their way, wanted the best for us, to shape us in their image. Merde!

NURSE: Yes, mmm-my father loved me in his way ...

H: Hmmm ... (?)

NURSE: My mother took care of it—of him.

H: Shit!

NURSE: We built a bridge and got over it. One must move on, as Mr. Cobb says.

H: Does he? Well, I moved on all right, left home and never stopped. On a sloppy track now, can't find my footing: wouldn't mind going back a bit, get back a few pieces of my old self.

NURSE: Yes. Time doesn't work like that.

H: No. Still, I moved on, job to job, war to war, wife to wife, big cat, big fish, big book.

NURSE: "Big man."

H: "Stranger than fiction." Not as big anymore. The me I created has run out of steam, if it ran on steam, or juice ... [holds blue bottle in one hand, whiskey in other, but doesn't drink]

NURSE: I believe so, but let's not further mix metaphor and reality.

H: Let's just try to get out of this mix-up. Do I have an even chance to come out the other side? Does it get me to a better place, or do I remain ... errant? [Nurse looks puzzled.] Wandering.

NURSE: Perhaps.

H: Shit.

NURSE: There does not appear to be any sure thing.

H: There's always a sure thing.

NURSE: Ah. Yes. Perhaps not drugs and convulsive shock; perhaps not drink and swearing; perhaps another way. I reserve judgment.

H: "Reserve"?

NURSE: [pause] Indefinitely. I try to keep you safe, as my job requires, but I believe the options are yours. Oh, yes, merde!, the options are yours.

H: Thank you for that.

NURSE: We understand each other. [Nurse takes blue bottle from H and carries to tray] Well, I've delivered ... more than my message, more than I should have. [Exit with tray stage right.]

[H sits and lowers head in hands. Knocking stage left.]

H: Come. [C & Mort enter.]

C: O.K. if I camp here awhile?

H: Sure. Keep me company. [drinks]

MORT: Mr. H, they're ready for you.

H: Huh!? Who's "they"? !

MORT: At the office.

H: How did they find me?! [confidentially to C] They're trying to catch me, get something on me.

MORT: No, no, the staff here. You remember. They're going to help you, getting things in order, forms and stuff.

H: Hah! covering their asses, in case, so to speak—

C: Oh, that kind of "case."

H:—if whatever's left of me when they finish complains about the parts that they lost. Forms, I'll bet!

MORT: But your family, ...

C: Families.

MORT: You need to be responsible, so—

H: Don't lecture me, you tenth-grade mop-pusher. I'll tell them what—screw their forms and screw them and screw you. [strides to wardrobe] My father taught me how to be "responsible." [places glasses on dresser and fastens his leather belt over robe preparing to leave]

MORT: [gestures] The conference room by the office.

H: [draws self up before mirror] I'll find them. And they'll find I don't take their kind of shit. Fuck 'em all.

[exit H, swearing Bleep, blankety blank blank bleepity Mort; Mort looks at C]

C: He doesn't mean it.

MORT: I think Mr. H has a problem.

C: Possibly more than one. We all have problems. That's why we're here. That's why we drink.

MORT: I mean the drink. It's not good for him, or people around him.

C: Now it doesn't seem to me he's drinking so much. [Mort's look contradicts him.] O.K., you've seen him more than I have.

MORT: Well it seems, along with the medicines he's—

C: "Drugs."

MORT:—drugs he's taking—drinking makes his ... moods worse.

C: Yeah, I can see his pain is emotional. I've got cancer. It's going to beat me, but drink beats the pain.

MORT: I'm sorry.

C: [more to self] Ernie's got lots of fears, and probably guilt—I can sympathize with that. Does drink help? Not so much anymore. [He]'s lost a lot, shadow of his old self ... maybe he drinks just to see a longer shadow. [Mort recoils slightly; C doesn't notice, thinking.] I hope you never end up where we are, but if you do, you'll see there are choices, and reasons for choices, you don't see now.

MORT: I just wish he wouldn't yell at me.

C: Don't listen.

MORT: Maybe they've got a "drug" for me to take not to do that.

C: Very likely. But whatever he yells, you hear, "darn it, I can't write, can't box-hunt-fish like I used to, can't make love, can't even enjoy the booze like I used to, but I can still make a row and fluster that poor son-of-a-gun Mort, who never did anything to deserve it."

MORT: O.K. Thanks Mr. Cobb.

C: You're welcome.

MORT: You're pretty smart for a ballplayer.

C: Thank you. I guess. You know, it's been a long while, but before I made it as a ballplayer I thought I should become a doctor.

MORT: A doctor!

C: That may have been my father's influence, that I thought that way, but I regret to this day that I never went to college. Get yourself through that night school. Mr. Hemingway will yell you the same, if he hasn't already.

MORT: O.K. I'll try.

C: Good. And never say die.

MORT: What!?

C: Get out! [Mort exits stage left; H re-enters stage right.] Ah.

H: I didn't sign anything, but I told them not to worry their litigious little heads. I've never ducked the consequences of anything I chose.

C: Main thing is you choose.

H: As far as possible. The prospects are closing in. As to when I'm gone, everyone will be taken care of. God knows I've hurt them and abandoned them many times in many ways, but never financially. Have made a good will to look after Bumby's and the other children's interests. And I always keep a certain amount of posthumous work around to pay the funeral expenses, et cetera. Now, need to take care of self.

C: Well, you're still writing.

H: Not good, or, got some good stuff but can't finish off. Or ... last year I went to Spain for Life, did a hundred and twenty thousand words, for a magazine! [does not notice that C has heard this before] They probably wanted twenty. I couldn't handle it. Hotch had to help me cut it down. I needed help. That's not me.

C: O.K.

H: Problems with safari book too. Well, problems with safari.

C: Hunting not good?

H: Hunting O.K., but flying not so. Nearly killed me.

C: You shot some of the big guns, .577?

H: Yes. Bagged a rhino.

C: Elephant?

H: No. That's an abomination. Killed lions, partly to help the Masai protect their cattle. Almost never without regret. And only shot males. Magnificent but lazy beasts. Like me. I work a few hours, try to produce a few good and true words, then fuck around and accomplish nothing the rest of the day. But, see, if I can't write those words ... About 200 words today, not even the league average.

C: Then you shoot yourself, because you can't hit .400 anymore ...

H: If I'm lucky.

C: Lucky?

H: If I shoot myself because of anything, for any reason, it means I still have reason. You can figure out why I'm here—because they dragged me out of a black pit where there were no choices, no

reason, no me. Fear and agony in command. Or as Professor Sliderule would say, chemistry had usurped the entire evolution of the human faculties. I had become the wounded hyena I saw in Africa, eating his own entrails.

C: Or, as Mort would say, "wow."

H: Here, now, I begin to feel I have, not very good, choices. When I'm up, it's a battle, but I never shied away from an unequal fight. The

Old Artificer versus Old Age. But when down, I feel there's such a pile-up of things to be done I can't get clear of the tangle, and the enemy's got me surrounded, and I can't keep fighting the rear-guard action if there's no "rear." No choices—it just "comes down to it."

C: You're still the skipper.

H: Sometimes, now, I feel I am; sometimes, just lost in those woods. Do I contradict myself?

C: Always have.

H: Or do myself contradict I?

C: Hmmm. Sounds like one of those whatchamacallit relationships ...

H: Anti-biotic. And how the hell do the quacks know which "I," which mentality or temperament, they'll end up volting out of me, and which myself they will leave, intact or fragmented? I realize the last few years—decades?—people said I changed, wasn't myself or wasn't the person they knew, especially current wife, thought I was confusing fact and fiction,—

C: Smudging the not-so-fine line?

H: Ha! Like the fine line between "brave" and "suicidal." The two may be highly contiguous. But I always knew the truth, and I knew that, when I wrote, my duty to the truth was as high as that of a priest of God, and I upheld it.

C: How many Germans did you kill?

H: Today? A hundred.

C: Today?

H: Today I tell you, I killed a hundred fascists, of all stripes, not including uncounted Krauts in their tin cans under the waters of the Gulf. But I never wrote about that; one doesn't write about one's own actions in the field.

C: You exaggerated, knowing that others would write it down.

H: And that others would clamor to set the record straight!

C: "Clamor to ..." A nice phrase. "The tumult and the shouting."

H: I was able to bring a little ballpark uproar to American literature.

C: Fiction. We have heard the voices raised both behind us and against us.

MORT [knocks, offstage]: Mr. Hemingway?

H: Come.

MORT: [enters] Nurse will be coming for you real soon.

[H&C regard Mort.]

H: "Ripeness is all." [Mort looks worried and puzzled.] Shakespeare. Timing is everything.

C: The Bard could have made a good hitting instructor.

H: No! We're not talking baseball now!

C: Nor boxing or bullfighting?

H: No! [sits]

MORT: [thinks it's a game] Or gambling?

[no response from H; C shakes his head, puts his arm around Mort and starts to lead him off]

MORT: [softly to C] You know that Ray Charles' cards song ...?

C: [nods, also softly] "Blackjack." I hear all that stuff on the radio. [looks back at H, who sits still, softly to Mort] How about Sinatra's ... ? [Exeunt.]

H: Time? [raises head, reaches for shot glass, looks at it, throws it across room, lowers head, takes pencil out of pocket, not looking at it rolls it in his fingers, puts it back.] Always said writing well was the hardest thing to do. I was wrong. Living without the ability is harder. [offstage PA paging Sister Florence] Dying is much easier. [H takes out a worn rabbit's foot, rubs with thumb. Derisively:] "Luck be a lady."

[H replaces rabbit's foot and remains still a few beats. Mort stealthily enters stage right, removes gun, and quietly exits stage left.]

H: La Puta. [H remains still a few more beats.] Bitch!

NURSE: [entering stage right] Excuse me? [retrieves shot glass]

H: [rises] You are always excused. Now, you're excused to go find that shifty orderly.

NURSE: What?

H: Mort. He's got a gun.

NURSE: What?! How?

H: It's not loaded, but, when he finds that out ... as we said, he's an enterprising little character. [C knocks stage right and enters.]

NURSE: I'll have to get the whole Clinic looking for him. I have no idea where he'd be.

H: He was just here, just took it; he left that way.

[Nurse hurries off stage left.]

C: Mort?

H: Yeah, oddball Mort. I had a shotgun under my mattress, which he somehow discovered and stole off with, thinking the old scout was going blind in the back of his head as well as the front.

C: He stolen other things, that we know of?

H: Nope. Don't think he'd lift a sheet of paper. But he has some strange obsession with death—"repulsion/attraction"? ... you notice he reacts to anything at all related?

C: Something screwy, now that you mention it, but I didn't make the connection.

H: A writer has to; details are his stock in trade. Occasionally helpful apart from art. I think that boy may be a danger to himself.

C: He may have left that way, but I noted where he keeps his things. [heads off stage right]

H: Grab your overcoat first!

C: Oh, right. [turns back] How'd they bring it in, closed, or broken, over an arm?

H: Closed, but we had a special-rigged coat.

C: Ah! I'll get it back somehow. Wish me luck.

H: [as C exits] Luck?! [calling after] It's not loaded! [pause] Might as well be talking to myself. Much ado about nothing. [unconsciously rubbing his rabbit's foot] Probably, if we're lucky. [aware of rabbit's foot, puts it back in pocket] Probably. [paces a few steps] Hope I haven't gotten the kid in trouble ... [smile/chuckle] more trouble. [pause] What did he think—? [walks over to dresser and opens top drawer, moves hand around in it] Oh [drawer slam covers obscenity]! [walks back to sit in chair and resumes head-in-hands pose; silence; PA announcement offstage, audible as something about Mort to come somewhere; H sits, fidgeting only slightly; C enters, deliberate footsteps, stage left, with overcoat across arm (barely possible there could be an open shotgun under it). H still not looking up:] You find it?

C: Yes. [C hangs overcoat in wardrobe.]

H: And the shells?

C: Yes. [leans over and whispers to H as Nurse enters stage right]

H: [looking up for first time]: It's O.K.

NURSE: We haven't found him yet.

H: Did you look in the chapel? [C looks at H, impressed.]

NURSE: Ahh. What happened?

H: [rises again] Mr. Cobb found the gun. He's taken care of it. It's safe now. Mort's safe.

NURSE: Where is it?

C: It's safe.

NURSE: Where?!

C: The fewer people know, the better.

NURSE: Ahh. And it's ... (?).

H&C: Not loaded.

C: [pointing off stage left] Chapel?

NURSE: Yes, that would be a shortcut: left to the end.

C: Thank you. [Exit.]

NURSE: Mr. Hemingway, I don't know what you were like before you came here.

H: In "the outside world."

NURSE: You could put it that way.

H: And you could possibly find that out in any number of popular periodicals and other unauthorized, but substantially accurate, publications, or perhaps within the pages of the floating file.

NURSE: Yes. That has been located.

H: Good, good, I'm very glad. Don't dust for fingerprints.

NURSE: Hmmm. As I was about to say, you are certainly capable of generating considerable agitation without leaving the confines of this clinic, or even getting out of your pajamas.

H: Probably better that than the other way 'round.

NURSE: [half smile] Anyway, I'm afraid someone may have called the police,—

H: [concerned] Local? [Nurse nods.] Now I assure you, you will never find that in my file.

NURSE:—and I imagine they cannot be stopped at this point, but—

H: Might be turned around pretty quickly.

NURSE: If you explained the current situation.

H: Safely stowed, not loaded. Or, never existed, phantom of over-active imagination, grossly exaggerated. Keep the true story short and spare.

NURSE: And not mentioning Mort.

H: No, no. [to self] Better than drugs.

NURSE: Eh?

H: After you. [as they exit] This more excitement than usual around here?

NURSE: Considerably, I assure you. [Exit stage right.]

H: [to self] Up and down, but maybe not finished yet. ... [Exit stage right.]

C: [beginning off stage left] ... not going to tell anyone, but if you ever do that again I'm gonna kill you.

MORT: [entering room pushed by C as though with gun in back] What, what?!

C: You know what. You were getting ready to shoot yourself.

MORT: No, no!

C: Why take the gun and the shells then?

MORT: I didn't know if the gun was loaded. [C stares at him. Admission:] Yes, but not after ... I got this job.

C: So ... ?

MORT: I thought Mr. H—you know, no doors on his room; and after I found the shells this morning, and I saw, a little bit, in his file.

C: About his father.

MORT: Shooting himself. [pause] I know, "confidential."

C: "A little knowledge" ... I imagine that was an interesting part. Did you read the medical notes? [Mort shakes head] Cracked bones, ruptured organs, dislocated shoulder, arm, eye problems, burns ...

MORT: Ooh. That's what you were saying, about why he drinks ...

C: That's why I drink. At first, it probably helped him with the physical pain. [winces and drinks] Then you get the psychological. They're still trying to figure out Ernie's mind.

MORT: Jim and Johnny [pointing to H's bottles]—"name your poison."

C: [restoppers flask] Jack. [pause] Then, there may come a time, the short names fall short. One turns to Rem-ing-ton or Winchester. [Mort recoils.] When you live in one of these rooms you'll see.

MORT: I did want to do something.

C: O.K., you tried. That puts Mort ahead of a lot of Jims and Johnnies. You can't keep us all alive; you don't want to. But—no doubt Nurse would have a better way of putting it—you keep something alive.

MORT: Thanks. And no.

C: Eh?

MORT: About Nurse.

C: O.K., probably, it just is sappy. [Mort punches C lightly on shoulder.] And I mean it about killing you! [repeat punch] O.K.!

[H enters from stage right.]

H: The felons return. [to Mort] What did you think you were up to?

MORT: Uh, ...

C: Turns out he was merely proposing to save you.

H: What!? [As Mort punches H lightly on shoulder, he processes it.] I don't need you, or anybody else, saving me. It's none of your—

C: He knows that now.

MORT: But,—

H: No "buts"! Just get your nosy little tail out of my room!

MORT: [leaving] O.K., yes, sir, Mr. H. [Exit. H fumes after him.]

C: "Nosy" "tail"?

H: Shuttup! I don't know why people think I can't take care of myself. All this interference ... shit!

C: [briefly holds up hands, surrender] You handle the gun alarm?

H: With nurse's help. Did you know her name was Barkley?

C: Really? [H shakes head and gazes blankly into distance as he ponders again the coincidence, but C interprets as doubting his statement] I may have been staring at her chest, but my eyes aren't good enough now to read her badge.

H: [not having listened] Some girl got hysterical, catching a glimpse of a big shiny gun flying down the hall, and called the police; fortunately they never had any details, so we spun 'em a tale. Your autographed bat came into it.

C: I'm sorry to have missed that.

H: Leave an autograph at the counter before you go. Don't write it to "Sergeant Lunkhead."

C: Usually I just sign for kids.

H: Here, I'll fix it up. [takes a sheet of paper and folds it in half; holds out hand to get C's green pen]

C: You're the author.

H: [as he writes] "In appreciation for gallant service
rendered by Chester PD
Autumn 1960

Ernest Hemingway

[holds out pen; C signs and keeps pen; H reads:]

Ty Cobb."

C: Accounts settled.

H: Should be all wrapped up. [inhale, exhale] They're still going to try to take care of me. God knows why. [absently/nervously refolds paper]

C: Perhaps, sometimes, only He does, but, you know, Mort—

H: Yeah, I know. ... I know. Kids.

C: "And most dogs." So, you trust them, or you handle it yourself.

H: Usually pays to trust nobody.

C: Handle important things yourself. For example, before I leave—

[As H&C talk, Mort & Nurse enter from opposite sides, Mort in his suit, Nurse in business suit, Nurse handing a small folder to H and Mort a large envelope to C. Nurse & Mort pull out and turn H's dresser, so back, painted to simulate fine wood with brass lettering,

SAINT MARY'S

HOSPITAL

near the top, faces audience. Nurse opens a middle drawer, from which Mort takes a black telephone and places it on top of "desk," behind which they stand. During scene Mort & Nurse nod or shake their heads to C&H, and their lips may move, but audience can hear no speech. H&C look through their packets.]

C:—I've paid extra, but it's worth it—they collect the originals of all reports, tests, orders, prescriptions and hand them over to me. I own and control them.

H: Hmmm. Good idea. I get a weekly accounting, itemization of every cent they charge me in this high-tech hoosegow. [wearing glasses, to Nurse] I'm charged 95 cents for phone calls? I only made local phone calls!

C: [to Mort] I said I wanted certified mail on this return envelope!

H: Well, they've got funny zones here. And what about laundry, I don't see the line for laundry.

C: Damn right twenty-eight cents isn't enough. More like a dollar twenty-eight if we've put a couple x-rays in here.

H: Well you should. They charge for laundry at the Ritz, and the Ritz can afford to do it gratis for what we pay them.

C: Alright, you do that! [shuffles through papers a bit] Everything else looks good. [placing envelope under arm, reaches in opposite pocket]

H: [putting glasses in robe pocket] Speaking of gratis, add a hundred bucks gratuity, share it among nurses and staff, Barkley's and Mort's level, not the doctors. And, here, [lays folded autograph sheet on "counter"] for them that also serve.

C: [handing Mort some $20s from a large wad] Here, for the staff, Mort and Mary, and Nurse B. You run a good shop here.

[Mort & Nurse replace phone, reverse dresser, and, just before they exit stage right, Nurse picks up C's folder, briefly glances at it, and stuffs the folded sheet and 20's into it.]

H: Always try to be careful and decent about money but like others to be careful.

C: Can't stand slipshod inattention and incompetence, because it looks like underhanded dishonesty, cheating—I don't mind an honest mistake.

H: It's not about the money.

C: No, it's about the "p" words.

H: "Principle."

C: "Paranoia."

H: Precisely.

C: Been working all my life to resent things a little less. Very tough battle. I'll stow this and return.

H: To see us off.

C: Right. Last rites. [pulls out and waves his flask as he exits stage right]

H: One for the road. [putting rabbit's foot in pocket, hand evidently runs into end of pencil] Ouch. [regards pencil as he takes it out; turns slowly to dresser and lays folder and pencil on top; turns and strolls toward front of stage, squinting towards audience] Kid's right; view's not bad. [puts on glasses as moves close to where window is] Interesting shadows. [closer; head/eyes move side to side] Light and dark; and light. The tallest trees get the last sun. [sights along arm, touching "window" with forefinger] And the first. Old Omar knew that. Of course, he was an astronomer as well as a poet and a rummy. "Ah, but" ... "computations"! "Ah, but my computations, people say, reduced the year to righter reckoning. Nay, 'twas only cutting from the calendar unborn tomorrow and dead yesterday." Close enough for an old war correspondent. An old ... dead, and all our yesterdays, ... but, tomorrow? [knocking stage right] .

NURSE: Mr. Hemingway.

H: Time?

NURSE: No, not quite. I wanted to check, if you were ready.

H: If I was prepared?

NURSE: [hesitantly] You could—

H: Physical courage, check. Moral courage, who needs it? morality is what you feel good after. Artistic courage, daring, see above: hold to what feels good and true.

NURSE: I see you are.

H: [to himself] Truer than if it really happened.

NURSE: Mrs. Hemingway is not visiting today?

H: Miss Mary? No. I'll give her a call. Afterwards, I guess.

NURSE: And I believe she has today talked by phone with one or more of your physicians.

H: Wouldn't surprise me. Smart girl. Amateur astronomer! Wants to take care of me, of course—I do appreciate that—but knows her limits. Probably knows mine better than I do myself, in some ways.

[becomes agitated] Has no understanding of my finances or affairs, or actions, especially any susceptible of misinterpretations—[a little frantic] completely innocent, without any guilty knowledge, never an accomplice or a fugitive.

NURSE: Yes, I understand, and—

H: Good.

NURSE: And she understands ...

H: What!?

NURSE: What we understand?

H: Ahh. I don't know. She'd like to make the choices, has made the choices, to prevent my making some choices, or choosing some ... paths.

NURSE: But she will accept your choice ...

H: "Accept"? Definitely not!

NURSE: She will accept as your choice, a choice she might not be able to accept?

H: She may accept that I choose [Nurse begins to smile.], but she would not ... Jesus, I feel,—what's the old insult, a weaponless ... ? mental battle ... ? A war of wits with an unarmed man.

NURSE: In the matter of wits, I would say you were far from unarmed, even in your present, semi- ...

H: Soused?

NURSE: even in a condition less healthy than it might be. And don't let Mrs. Hemingway make you think otherwise.

H: Mmm.

NURSE: Well, don't let anyone.

H: Myself included.

NURSE: I suppose that also gets a bit convoluted.

H: No, no, that's clear. I don't want to turn into the people I've always fled and resisted, who would tell me I had to do this or could not do that. [half smile] I don't want to become my father or my mother.

NURSE: Drink to that.

[knocking stage right]

H: Come! [C and Mort enter.] All assembled, huh? [to Mort] What now?!

MORT: [holds up dusting rag] Oh, you know.

C: I'm leaving.

H: I see. [looks at Nurse, who nods] Me too. [He cinches his belt one hole tighter.]

NURSE: Farewell, Mr. Cobb.

C: Guess I don't need to say, "take care."

[C&H half-smile at each other.]

H: So long, you old son of a bitch.

C: Bless you, young man.

[H waves off blessing/good-bye with shot glass, from which he drinks.]

H: Don't take any wooden stock certificates.

C: [as Nurse & H exit stage left] Don't take any called third strikes.

[C goes to wardrobe, takes and puts on overcoat.]

MORT: [shivers, pause] D'you think he'll go down swinging?

C: Oh, well ... [upbeat-positive for Mort] always has. Maybe you'll be around to find out. I gotta go.

MORT: God bless, Mr. Cobb.

C: Thanks, kid. [takes out flask] You too. Here's to you, Mort [quick swig as he moves off], and to "old Ernie Hemorrhoid, the poor man's Pyle."

[pause, Mort puzzled, while C exits stage right]

MORT: Poor man.

[Mort is rubbing a silver dollar in one hand; he puts it in his pocket. The lights flicker and then steady a bit dimmer.]

MORT: [looking out window.] Gets dark earlier every day. [wipes a spot - coordinate with H's forefinger]

[As he uses rag to dust window sill and frame, Mort whistles: Our boys will shine tonight, (breath) our boys will shine; (breath) Our boys will shine tonight—interrupted on the high note by a muffled concussive sound offstage left (could be a shotgun blast or the sound in an old movie when they throw the main electric switch—or a large dictionary dropped flat on a wooden floor) and a brief flash of light. Mort holds his head. Lights out. Ten seconds. Stage and house lights up, Mort and Nurse front-center for quick bows. Mort & Nurse snap fingers at wings, C&H enter for bows.]

* * *

Questions, suggestions, permission to produce:

Richard Jesson 415-668-1510

dpjbj@sbcglobal.net

About the Author

Dick Jesson is a retired hitting instructor living in San Francisco. He studied English and American literature at University of California, Berkeley, and University of California, Riverside.